FUNDAMENTALS OF TRADING

What you need to know before operating

Oliver Nuñez Velasco

*To crazies who decide to invest

in the securities markets.*

Introduction

When we are interested in the financial markets and invest some of our money in them, the first word that comes to mind is trader.

Our brain assimilates the word trader, with a person who earns money and immediately we want to be a trader, and we want to start making money from now.

To achieve this, besides the necessary expertise, we need to learn another set of values.

This book is intended to lay the groundwork, the foundation, so that together with the technical learning you have acquired, avoid errors in your operations.

THE TRADING

THE MARKET

THE DIRECTION OF THE PRICES

TECHNICAL ANALYSIS

CHART ANALYSIS

MATCHING SIGNS

THE OPERATIONS

THE STRATEGY

RISK MANAGEMENT

THE OBJECTIVES

DISCIPLINE

PSYCHOLOGY

THE LOST

THE STOPS

TO RESUME

THE TRADING

The trading involves buying and selling stocks. Is, therefore, operate in the securities market.

The trading is based on three pillars:

- Monetary Management. Is to calculate the risk that we are willing to assume.

- Psicotrading. It is based on use in psychology and self-knowledge to avoid making mistakes and learning from the mistakes made in the past.

- Technical Analysis and Graphic Analysis. It consists in applying the technical expertise to study the market and to decide the entry and exit points.

Trading is an exercise in technique, practice and discipline. All this within a behavior with a strong psychological component.

To be trader is not only necessary to have a inicial capital to start investing, but must also be taken technical training in order to make a comprehensive and detailed analysis of the values on which it is intended to invest (define a method of investment), and we must have a psychological rigor.

To make trading, we must have discipline, rigor and always follow rules.

Among the trading´s rules, it is very important to include: "to know how to stop losses and let profits run."

As for the psychological aspect, we have to keep in mind that it is impossible to eliminate emotions. It is unnatural.

Another very important aspect is to be clear that the market is constantly changing and you are unchanging, so you must be constant.

Therefore, to be a good trader you must:

- Know. Is to acquire the technical knowledge necessary.
- know how. Is to apply the knowledge acquired successfully.
- Be. Is the experience and psychological rigor.

THE MARKET

The market is a physical or virtual place (trading platforms), where a price or share price varies constantly according to supply and demand.

It is a board game or battle between the bulls forces (bulls) and bearish forces (bears).

Players are divided into two groups: professional and amateur.

As in any game, there are winners and losers. It is governed by a fundamental rule: "to win others must lose." The benefits do not come out of nowhere.

Therefore one must not fall into the trap of the market. The market looks to be attractive. Professionals attempt to take money from others professionals, but mostly from non-professional players.

When we are not professional investors, we have to value our money enormously and hence avoid operations that make us leave the market and make us lose all our money.

Once we decided to enter the market, we should be aware of what we do, where we are going and where we want to endure.

THE DIRECTION OF THE PRICES

The hardest thing to do when you want to do trading, is to guess which way the price is going to evolve.

When we set our strategy, we use all the tools at our disposal. One is technical knowledge.

We can establish the following guidelines to help us guess the price´s direction.

These guidelines are:

- Define the line of least resistance. As happens in nature, where the water flows through the areas that generate less resistance, in the stock market, prices move down the line of least resistance. The support, resistance and congestion zones are areas where the price tends to slow or stop.
- Defining the value. It is the area between two moving averages, a fast and a slow. In an uptrend, the price rises to leave the area of value to a point of maximum euphoria when many investors begin to regret having brought the price to such an extent. Then common sense returns the value to the area. In a downtrend, the price is lowered

away from the area of value to a point of maximum pessimism.

- Set the surround channel. The sequence of the points of maximum euphoria and pessimism, make the surround channel.
- Divergences. It is defined as the opposite behavior between price and indicator. Represent entry opportunities.
- Inertia. If the trend is up, chances are good that the price movement is upward; if bearish, means that most of the movements can be downloaded.
- Use technical and graphical analysis.

TECHNICAL ANALYSIS

Technical analysis attempts to identify patterns of price behavior in order to detect and anticipate trends, which uses graphics that represent the evolution of prices over time and statistical indicators.

The objective is to predict the future evolution of prices from the behavior that prices have had in the past. To achieve this, technical analysis is based on the following principles:

Prices evolve according to guidelines.

The technical analysis uses the information provided by the market to predict trend changes.

Markets are repetitive: the past is repeated in the future.

The markets are fractal; the chart's figures are repeated at any time, "frame", which is analyzed.

In view of the above, technical analysis tries to anticipate trend changes; the end of an existing tendency and the beginning of the next.

Since the two pillars of technical analysis are charts and statistical indicators, reliability is probabilistic and not accurate. Otherwise, we'd all be millionaires.

CHART ANALYSIS

The analysis of price charts is critical to try to guess the direction of price´s development.

With the analysis of the graphs we can determine:

1 -. Trends contributions.

2 -. Identify which movements may occur if these trends will change.

. 3 - Fix support and resistance.

4 -. Setbacks or movements against the main trend.

When analyzing a price chart we can establish the following sequence:

1. Draw a moving average. This line allows us to determine the trend of value.

2. Charting a surround channel. They are two lines between which the price is moving.

3. We add indicators like volume, which indicates the interest of investors on value.

4. We add technical indicators.

MATCHING SIGNS

When we do trading, we need to consider the concept of matching signals.

Our chances of success are based on statistical probabilities, so that when several signals coincide at the same point and in the same direction, reinforce each other and increase our chances of success.

It is good, operate in points where there are many signals because it will increase the chances of success, but although there are many signals that match, can never have a 100% safety on the future development of the prices, which must be taken into account in the control risks incurred by each investor.

THE OPERATIONS

When operating, we can distinguish between short or long term operations. And based on this we can define the following:

Long in favour of trend

It is a transaction in which you buy, in a bull market, on the rebound on support and we sell when the price starts to drop.

Short in favour of trend

In a market with a bearish trend may be sold when the price reaches resistance and it stops.

Long against the trend

Is to harness the corrections that occur in the main trend.

If the market is bearish, we can buy when the prices reaches an important support to take advantage if the price rebounds.

Short against the trend

Is to sell to take advantage of corrections of uptrends.

THE STRATEGY

No one can predict the future and no one without some kind of reasoning can predict the direction in which the price will evolve.

What we should do is raise as much as possible the chances of hitting the direction of evolution of the price.

The price moves as a result of supply and demand. Sometimes this movement can be analyzed and used to our advantage. To do this we must use all the expertise, practical experience and psychology, and translate them into a strategy.

The strategy is defined as a set of rules, behaviors and procedures designed to select and manage the portfolio.

The strategy should always be respected, because is your investment plan.

There is no reliable investment strategy to 100% and is not the same for all investors.

Therefore, the investment strategy should be tailored to each investor (each investor must define its own strategy) including risks and profitability targets.

The strategy should never be a fixed and strict plan, but can be changing. Must adapt to the circumstances at all times.

RISK MANAGEMENT

We must keep in mind that we operate correctly when we manage risk well.

Managing risk is to know the risk, for which we must know learn how to lose.

We can use the following cycle:

Before operating. We have to watch the market to choose the entry point.

During operating. We need to manage the operation, detecting exit points.

After operating. We need an analysis of what happened, whether we have obtained benefits as if we have incurred losses.

At all stages of the cycle, our tools are technical knowledge, practical experience and psychology.

When we are managing risk, we should not enter the market thinking about what I can earn but what I can lose.

A simple method is to not accept more than a certain percentage of loss of our investment.

This will set a fixed value for our losses. This fixed value can go modifying it in various ways:

• Periodically. Every so often we calculate the percentage of allowable loss of our investment. If our investment has increased, we increase the risk and if you have decreased, the risk decreases.

• Maintaining the fixed value and calculating a variable. The allowable loss value of our investment is maintained and we calculate a percentage of allowable loss for the benefits to be obtained is calculated. If losses are greater than the benefits, we apply the fixed value.

• Depending on the account. If the account grows, we increase the risk percentage. Is to assimilate the benefits to investment. We believe we have more capital and we can increase the risk margin.

Another method to manage risk is to modify the percentage loss that we want to assume, based on the profits or losses of each operation.

If we get benefits, we increase the percentage of risk and if we get losses, decrease the percentage.

Consider the following example:

Initial capital	$ 50.000,00		
Risk		2,00%	$ 1.000,00
Periodic review			
1. Benefits	$ 2.000,00		
Available capital	$ 52.000,00		
Risk		2,00%	$ 1.040,00
2. Losses	$ -2.000,00		
Available capital	$ 48.000,00		
Risk		2,00%	$ 960,00
Fixed and variable value			
1. Benefits	$ 2.000,00		
Available capital	$ 50.000,00		
Risk		2,00%	$ 1.000,00
Irrigation for benefits		1,00%	$ 20,00
Total risk			$ 1.020,00
2. Losses	$ -500,00		
Available capital	$ 50.000,00		
Risk		2,00%	$ 1.000,00

Review of the account

1. Benefits	$ 2.000,00		
Available capital	$ 50.000,00		
Account value	$ 52.000,00		
Risk		2,00%	$ 1.040,00
2. Losses	$ -500,00		
Available capital	$ 50.000,00		
Risk		2,00%	$ 1.000,00

Revision according to profit/loss

Available capital	$ 50.000,00		
Risk		2,00%	$ 1.000,00
Result operation 1	$ 2.000,00		
Increased risk for operation		0,10%	$ 2,00
Total risk			$ 1.002,00
Result operation 2	$ 1.500,00		
Increased risk for operation		0,10%	$ 1,50
Total risk			$ 1.003,50
Result operation 3	$ -2.500,00		
Increased risk for operation		0,10%	$ -2,50
Total risk			$ 1.001,00
Result operation 4	$ 5.000,00		
Increased risk for operation		0,10%	$ 5,00
Total risk			$ 1.006,00

THE OBJECTIVES

It is very important to set objetives to achieve with your investments.

The first and last objetive is to keep survival. Being in the market, is be inside the game board and therefore able to continue playing. Means to be alive.

The scale of objectives that we could define might be:

First objective. Acquiring knowledge.

Second objective. Gaining experience and confidence.

Third objective. Learning from the successes and mistakes.

Fourth objective. Get benefits.

Fifth objective. Increase benefits.

DISCIPLINE

Once we decided to enter the market, we must be disciplined.

All disciplined behavior is based on four pillars:

- Technical knowledge. The study of technical analysis allows us to establish the tools to operate.

- Practical experience. Each operation is associated with a success or failure, of which we learn for the future.

- Risk management. It is very important to be clear what we are willing to lose.

- Psychology. At all times we must learn to control our emotions and impulses.

Being able to maintain proper discipline is synonymous with success.

PSYCHOLOGY

The psychological aspect when we making trading is as important as the analysis of price charts or technical analysis.

We can find a lot of literature about it that allow us to acquire knowledge needed to start trading.

But who helps to train the psychological aspect?. We must be ourselves, the teacher and the student.

The first thing to learn before operating is: "You have to know how to lose." Humans are used to not know how to lose. Greed is tucked deep within their genetic structure. We are born being greedy.

We must isolate and control our emotions. Our main goal is to survive in the market.

We expiration date depending on our portfolio management and how we operate. This expiration date will be earlier when there are more emotions in our trading.

It is very important to learn from mistakes and successes. Trading in the stock market, is to repeat purchase and sale, with similar characteristics, so, we must use the past experience.

History repeats itself. At the dawn of mankind, Hecráclito said that that it is no possible to bathe twice in the same river, because different waters flow towards you at all times.

The same happens in the stock markets, operations seem to be repeated with similar characteristics, so we should use that.

They are not exactly alike, but they are much similar to what happened in the past.

You have to know how to lose and remove stage fright. The best trader in the world do not win at all its operations. When an operation goes wrong, you have to assume it.

Keep in mind that your greatest enemy is you. Therefore you must avoid to justify losses and try to survive in the market. Do not do more damage than necessary. If you have lost money, is not enough damage?.

If you've managed to survive in the market, returns to control your emotions, learn from the mistake, look repeat opportunities and remove the stage fright.

At the end, is a cycle that is repeated constantly and has the following main goal: trying to make money to survive.

When we say that the worst enemy of the investor is not the other players on the board (investors), is probably supported by psychological studies.

There is a defense mechanism of our brain called "cognitive dissonance".

This mechanism becomes our worst enemy when trying to operate and mask a painful reality.

When we win we are happy and when we lose it is very difficult to accept. The human mind alters the perception of things to make them more palatable.

We try to justify past decisions. It is a defense mechanism to be more to taste ourselves. This is a mistake in trading. If you take a decision and went wrong, that's it, it's over. Hence the importance of stop-loss.

We must eliminate the psychological stress of choices when they go wrong.

It is very easy for our brain and our ego will close positions with benefits and yet it is very difficult to accept a position that it generates more losses and close the position.

We must move away from our brains all sorts of emotions when trading. Fear, elation, pride and stubbornness are examples of feelings that we must move away from our brain.

Fear prevents us from taking appropriate investment decisions on points of entry into the market.

The euphoria when we get the profit makes us lose respect for the market and other investors, thinking we are the smartest in the class.

Pride can make us lose a lot of money. Not accept a loss, leads to erroneous decisions that can chain more losses and exit the market at the end losing the main objective: survival.

The obstinacy and stubbornness to remedy past mistakes without reasoning necessary, lead to immature decisions.

To combat those feelings we can follow the following rules:

• Operate in quiet moods.

• Be focused when making decisions.

- Do not make hasty decisions. Decisions must be matured, besides being confirmed with the technical knowledge and practical experience.

- Do fight against the market. The market always wins. It is a simple statistical question. You are just one and the market tends to infinity. For very fierce bear or bull you are, the market is full of a bunch of bears and bulls as fierce as you. A soldier can never beat an army.

- Do not think you've failed to win.

- The market always gives you another chance.

THE LOST

The loss is the lack or deprivation of what is owned. In the stock market, the loss is the decline of wealth or economic heritage.

It is vital when operating in the market understand that losses are inherent to trading.

The explanation is simple. Whenever decisions are made, there is from a statistical standpoint a percentage chance of making a mistake.

An error in trading is synonymous with loss.

However, despite the losses represent a failure of the decisions, we must be able to learn from mistakes (losses).

When you have a losing trade, first thing to do is to relativize the problem. Relativize is to give the importance it deserves, the world does not end.

Second, once we have relativized the problem, we objectively analyze why we made the mistake and we lost.

Objectively analyze the losses is to see what we did wrong and why. It can be due to a failure of our strategy and we have not been disciplined.

It can be due to a failure of our psychology, experience or knowledge.

The conclusion we get after relativization and analysis is the basis for not repeat the same mistake.

THE STOPS

The stops are price's safe level of sell, placed below the current price, in the case of long positions. Intended to limit losses when the price drops. In this case the stop is called stop-loss.

Therefore, if the stop-loss is placed properly, no operation will cause more losses than we want when we set the stop-loss.

The other stop, called stop-gain is used to ensure a profit and avoid the possibility of the price to fall back to the point of purchase (or below it) and the unrealized gain to be had is lost in that position.

When set the stop as prices evolve, the stop will be moved in the direction of price's movement if we can be favored.

If this is a stop-loss and price rises so that we can move said stop above the purchase price, the stop will be stop-gain and we can have benefit and we can protect the gains with the new stop.

The criteria that we can be used to place a stop are:

Using the latest maximum or relative minimum. Is to place the stop loss below the last relative maximum or relative minimum, using a safe margin to prevent false signals of break of these levels and avoid that we can take off the market.

A false signal occurs when the price breaks the stop with for very little room to resume after the previous movement. Here a discrepancy arises: the larger the margin over the lower stop is the probability that the market take us because there has been a false signal, but the greater the loss in case of rupture of the stop.

Using support and resistance. If we are in bullish positions the stop-loss is placed under a nearby support and bearish positions on a close above resistance. This method is based on belief in the strength of support and resistance.

Using moving averages. The averages serve as support and resistance so the method is similar to above. In a buying operation, the stop-loss will be executed when the price crosses down to the moving average, while a bearish operation, the stop loss will be executed when the price crosses up to the moving average.

The downside is how media we have to use because the averages do not anticipated trends but confirm trends, and therefore do not know if the market will break the average.

Fixed percentage of the purchase price. It is set at the time of purchase the maximum amount allowable losses.

Minimum / maximum the latest X sessions. Similar to the last case concerning minimum or maximum, but here you take the higher or lower value of the prices for X sessions.

The main drawback of using stops, apart from their improper placement, is the psychological part of their use, since all stop-loss if makes, it takes losses and we have to accept that we made a mistake with our operation.

To compensate for the psychological part, it is best to set a maximum allowable loss, which can be fixed in 1-2% of the total capital invested.

It would apply the method of section 4; assume at the time of purchase, the level of risk (of losing money) on our investment.

The problem that may be associated with stop-loss is that the price falls below it and not skip us. This is due to the appearance of voids, which are price ranges where there is no supply or demand and therefore do not intersect operations. Nobody wants to buy / sell at those prices.

Suppose we have a stop loss set to a value X. The share price begins to fall and from X +1 to X-2 a hole is formed; no consideration for us to sell in X. The price is now in X-2, whereby we assumed loss with stop-loss, plus -2 (difference between X and X-2).

TO RESUME

To summarize, you can set the following premises:

In the stock markets are the smartest people we face and what they want, our money.

There are always winners and losers.

It's a fight between bulls and bears.

Trading is an exercise in technique, practice and discipline.

Learn lose.

Know win.

The first and last aim is to reach survival.

Let run profits and limit your losses.

It is impossible to guess 100% of the time.

No look perfect scenarios.

History repeats itself.

So important is the input as the output.

We have to be disciplined.

The strategy must always be respected.

The technical and graphical analysis are weapons in our favor.

We must isolate our emotions.

Your worst enemy is you.

You have to remove stage fright.

You have to manage irrigation

Always use stops-loss.

To succeed we must always remember the above expressions.

Are simple phrases that will not teach us points of entry into the market, amounts to invest, percentage of risk to take, where to place our stops-loss, ... but they help us enormously to have controlled the psychological aspect.

www.ingramcontent.com/pod-product-compliance
Lightning Source LLC
Chambersburg PA
CBHW072046190526
45165CB00018B/1849